10/4/16

LEVEL
1
YOU READ · I READ

Day and Night

Shira Evans

NATIONAL GEOGRAPHIC

Washington, D.C.

How to Use This Book

Reading together is fun! When older and younger readers share the experience, it opens the door to new learning. As you read together, talk about what you learn.

This side is for a parent, older sibling, or older friend. Before reading each page, take a look at the words and pictures. Talk about what you see. Point out words that might be hard for the younger reader.

This side is for the younger reader.

As you read, look for the bolded words. Talk about them before you read. In each chapter, the bolded words are:
Chapter 1: times of day • Chapter 2: action words
Chapter 3: describing words • Chapter 4: action words
• Chapter 5: describing words

At the end of each chapter, do the activity together.

Table of Contents

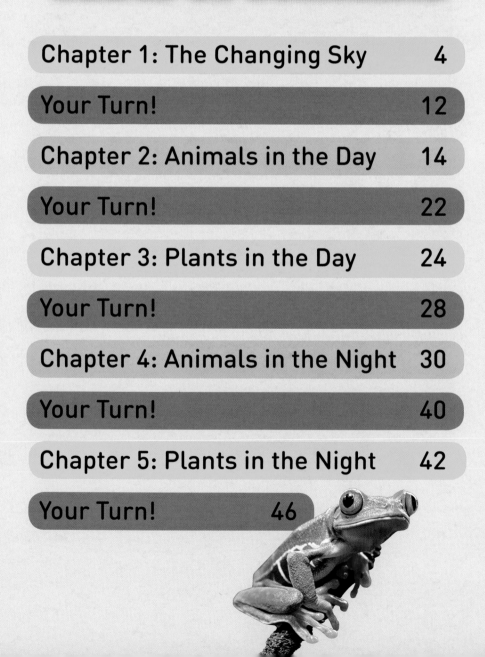

CHAPTER 1

The Changing Sky

It's early morning, and the sky is changing. It's **dawn,** and the colors in the sky turn from black to purple and red.

Now the sky turns from red to orange. It's still **dawn.**

Soon the sky will turn blue.

As the sun rises higher, it lights up the land. The water and trees start to become brighter and clearer. **Daytime** is coming.

It's **daytime** now. The sun is high in the sky.

The sky is blue, and the clouds are white.

 Now it's late afternoon, and the sun has moved across the sky. It makes long shadows on the land. Day is beginning to turn to **dusk.**

It's **dusk.** The sun is setting.

The sky changes color again. Soon it will be night.

The sun has set. Darkness falls across the land. The sun is rising on the other side of the world. There, it is daytime. But here, it is **nighttime.**

At **nighttime,** the sky is full of stars. The sun is gone. Now the moon shines bright.

YOUR TURN!

Tell what time of day each photo shows. Use the sun as a hint.

Times of Day

dawn   daytime

dusk   nighttime

1

CHAPTER 2

Animals in the Day

Above the ocean, the sun **rises.** Soon it's high enough in the sky to brighten the water. A school of fish starts to become active.

As the sun **rises,** it fills
the water with more light.
It's now dawn. The fish look
for food.

It's noon, and the sun **shines** brightly overhead. A group of monkeys swings through the trees. The monkeys have been awake since sunrise and have a lot of energy to play.

 The sun **shines** on the monkeys. It makes them warm.

The monkeys have played for hours. Now they will take a nap.

 It's late afternoon on the savanna, and the sun starts to **drop.** An ostrich looks out across the land.

The sun **drops** lower in the sky. The sky turns orange and red.

The ostrich must eat before the sky gets too dark.

The sun **sinks** lower in the sky.
It's dusk. A flock of starlings comes
together, forming a black cloud
in the sky.

The birds are safe in the flock. They keep each other warm.

They sing until the sun **sinks** out of sight.

YOUR TURN!

Play a game with a friend. Tell what time of day each photo shows. Then have your friend tell what each animal does during the day.

1

ANSWERS: 1. late afternoon; the ostrich looks for food. 2. dawn; the fish look for food. 3. dusk; the birds flock and sing. 4. noon; the monkeys play and then sleep.

4

3

2

CHAPTER 3

Plants in the Day

YOU READ

The sun shines **brightly** overhead. A field of sunflowers looks cheerful and yellow in the sunshine. The flowers turn to follow the sun across the sky.

That helps them collect light from the sun. They use the light to make energy.

 At night, the sun does not shine. The flowers droop.

They will open again tomorrow. The sun will shine **brightly** again then.

It's daytime, and a lotus flower opens **wide.** Its strong smell and pretty color attract a dragonfly. The dragonfly will get food inside the flower.

The dragonfly needs the flower to be **wide** open. That way it can find food.

When night falls, the flower will close.

YOUR TURN!

Pretend to be these animals and plants during the day. Act out what each is doing.

Run like an ostrich.

Swim like a fish.

Follow the sun like a flower.

Play like a monkey.

Fly like a bird.

CHAPTER 4

Animals in the Night

YOU READ

In the dark, hungry lions stalk the land. The sun set hours ago, and the moon provides the only light. The lions **watch** and wait.

A lion can see in the dark.

This helps it **watch** for food in the night.

YOU
READ

In the dark, an elf owl peeks out of its nest in a Saguaro cactus. The temperature has cooled, and now the owl can hunt. It **listens** for signs of prey. Soon it will set out in search of food.

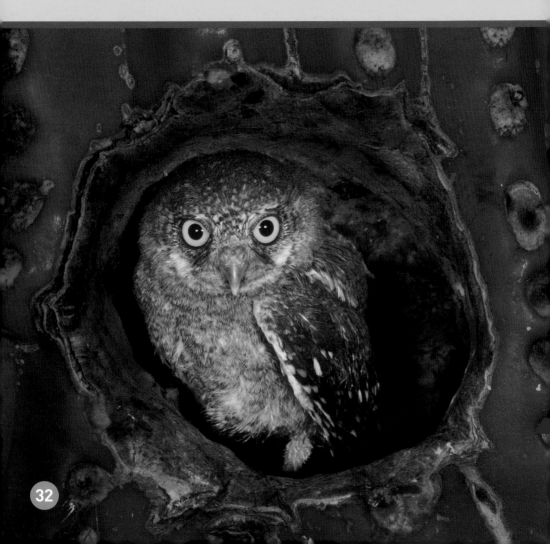

 Most owls can see well at night. This owl **listens,** too.

It can find food even when it can't see.

In the dark, a red-eyed tree frog blinks its big eyes open. It's hungry.

The frog sits quietly and waits as it **searches** for food. Suddenly, it spots movement on a leaf.

 The frog is quick. It catches its food.

But it's still hungry. The frog **searches** for food all night.

In the dark, a raccoon wakes up. It **peeks** out into the night as it looks and listens. All seems safe. It's time to leave the den and hunt. The raccoon will use its excellent sight and hearing to find food in the dark.

 The raccoon trots down to the river. It **peeks** into the water.

There's a fish here!

YOU READ

In the dark, a termite mound starts to glow. It's not the termites, though. On the tower, hundreds of glowworms light up the night. They are glowing to **attract** food.

The glowworms' lights shine bright. This **attracts** their food.

It makes their food come right to them! Now it's easy for the glowworms to eat.

glowworm

YOUR TURN!

What sense does each animal use most to get around in the dark? What senses do you use in the dark?

Word Bank

see   hear

1

CHAPTER 5

Plants in the Night

Darkness falls, and a balsa flower opens wide. Inside is a sweet liquid. Many **nocturnal,** or nighttime, animals are attracted to its scent, and they come to drink.

The flower closes in the day. It will open again at night.

Nocturnal animals sleep in the day, too. They will wake up again at night.

In the dark
forest, a group
of fungi gives off an
eerie, **glowing,** green light.

The fungi only glow at night, but they
couldn't make their light without the
daytime sunlight.

During the day, the fungi store the sun's light.

At night, they turn the stored light into the glowing light.

YOUR TURN!

Which activities do you do in the day? Which do you do at night? Tap the day side or night side of the tree as you read each activity.

sleep

see sun

see stars

see moon

swim

read

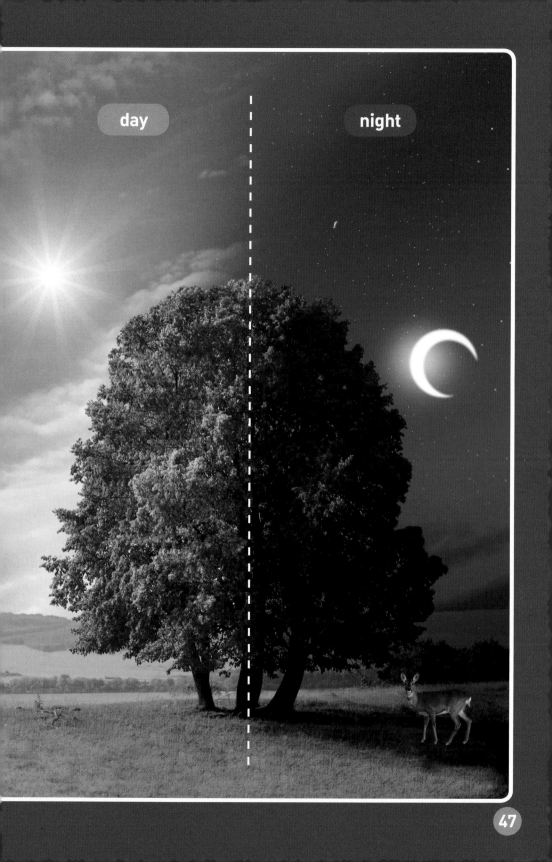

day

night

For Sam and Alex, whose love of science and nature continues to inspire me. —S.E.

Art Director: Amanda Larsen

The author and publisher gratefully acknowledge the expert literacy review of this book by Susan B. Neuman, Ph.D., professor of early childhood and literacy education, New York University.

Illustration Credits

GI = Getty Images; MP = Minden; NGC = National Geographic Creative; NPL = Nature Picture Library; SS = Shutterstock
COVER: LilKar/SS; (deer), Eric Isselee/SS; 1, Rolf Nussbaumer/NPL; 2 (UP LE), Jane Tregelles/Alamy; 2 (UP RT), Fotosearch Value/GI; 2 (LO-A), Klein and Hubert/NPL; 2 (LO-C), perspectivestock/SS; 2 (LO-E), Chris Gomersall/Alamy; 2 (LO-D), Yukihiro Fukuda/NPL; 2 (LO-B), David Doubilet/NGC; 3, iStock.com/Brandon Alms; 4-5, Vincent Grafhorst/MP; 6, Stephen Belcher/MP; 7, Manoj Shah/GI; 8, Theo Allofs/MP; 9, Michele Westmorland/GI; 10-11, Michael Nichols/NGC; 12, iStock.com/Wolfgang Filser; 13 (UP), iStock.com/GooDween 123; 13 (CTR), iStock.com/Andreas Vitting; 13 (LO), iStock.com/Martin Maun; 14, David Doubilet/NGC; 15, Brian J. Skerry/NGC; 16, Yukihiro Fukuda/NPL; 17, Yukihiro Fukuda/NPL; 18, Paul Bruins Photography/GI; 19 (LE), Vincent Grafhorst/MP; 19 (RT), Michel and Christine Denis-Huot/MP; 20-21, Gail Johnson/SS; 22, Paul Bruins Photography/GI; 23 (UP), Brian J. Skerry/NGC; 23 (LO LE), Gail Johnson/SS; 23, Yukihiro Fukuda/NPL; 24, perspectivestock/SS; 25, Jose A. Bernat Bacete/GI; 26-27, Jane Tregelles/Alamy ; 27 (INSET), Fotosearch Value/GI; 28 (LE), Klein and Hubert/NPL; 28 (RT), David Doubilet/NGC; 29 (UP), perspectivestock/SS; 29 (LO LE), Yukihiro Fukuda/NPL; 29 (LO RT), Chris Gomersall/Alamy Stock Photo/Alamy; 30, Frans Lanting/NGC; 31, Michael Nichols/NGC; 32, Cultura RM/Art Wolfe Stock/GI; 33, Tom Vezo/MP; 34, Photolukacs/SS; 35, Stephen Dalton/NPL; 36, Thomas Lazar/NPL; 37, Rolf Nussbaumer/NPL; 38, Ary Bassous; 39, David J. Slater/Alamy ; 40, Rick and Nora Bowers/Alamy; 41 (UP), reptiles4all/SS; 41 (CTR), John Cancalosi/NPL; 41 (LO), Brigitta Moser/GI; 42-43, Christian Ziegler/MP; 44-45, Nick Garbutt/MP; 46 (UP LE), K. Miri Photography/SS; 46 (UP CTR), jeka84/SS; 46 (UP RT), sripfoto/SS; 46 (LO LE), Somchai Som/SS; 46 (LO CTR), AlexRoz/SS; 46 (LO RT), studioVin/SS; 47, LilKar/SS; 47 (deer), Eric Isselee/SS

Library of Congress Cataloging-in-Publication Data

Names: Evans, Shira, author. | National Geographic Society (U.S.)
Title: Day and night / by Shira Evans.
Description: Washington, D.C. : National Geographic, [2016] | Series: National Geographic readers | Audience: Ages 2-5.
Identifiers: LCCN 2015045640| ISBN 9781426324703 (pbk. : alk. paper) | ISBN 9781426324710 (library binding : alk. paper)
Subjects: LCSH: Day--Juvenile literature. | Night--Juvenile literature. | Earth (Planet)--Rotation--Juvenile literature.
Classification: LCC QB633 .E93 2016 | DDC 525.35--dc23
LC record available at https:// lccn.loc.gov_2015045640

National Geographic supports K–12 educators with ELA Common Core Resources. Visit natgeoed.org/commoncore for more information.

Printed in the United States of America
16/WOR/1